D1603531

HOW TO LIVE LIKE
The Little Prince

HOW TO LIVE LIKE
The Little Prince

a grown-up's guide to
rediscovering imagination,
adventure, and awe

STÉPHANE GARNIER

TRANSLATED FROM THE FRENCH
BY REBECCA LEFFLER

CHRONICLE PRISM

First published in the United States of America in 2022 by Chronicle Books LLC.
Originally published in France in 2021 by Éditions de l'Opportun as *Agir et penser comme Le Petit Prince.*

Library of Congress Cataloging-in-Publication Data available.

ISBN 978-1-7972-1573-0

Manufactured in China.

English translation by Rebecca Leffler.
Design by Brooke Johnson.
Typesetting by Maureen Forys, Happenstance Type-O-Rama.
Typeset in Arno Pro, Brandon, and Rossanova Pro.

10 9 8 7 6 5 4 3 2

To Galou and Sanou,
dear Little Princes.

CONTENTS

To . . . you.

Because giving a book is an act of love.

This book is yours.

This book is perhaps an opportunity to deliver a message or to give a gift to someone you love. A personal message is worth much more than an author's dedication.

I dedicate this book to: _____

_____

_____

_____

foreword

MANY STUDIES HAVE INSISTED ON reading between the lines of *The Little Prince*. A desire to decode certain symbols, or to search for hidden meanings that Antoine de Saint-Exupéry slipped into his book makes sense, but that manner of reading *The Little Prince* is a very different approach from mine.

I wanted to focus on the Little Prince himself, on his words, his doubts, his quest, the values and dreams he holds dear, and the ideas he shares.

What is essential in a book is not only what the author wanted us to understand, but also what we want to understand. *The Little Prince* exemplifies a way of approaching life that is much different from that of most people. I wanted to focus on the character of the Little Prince, to figure out his motivations and the driving forces of his life, to discover how this little man, this magician, has had such an influence on so many of us, at one time or another in our lives, whatever our age, culture, or language, and has moved, touched, fascinated us, and made us dream.

Finally, while rereading the book, something I had not done for a long time, I ended up adopting his thoughts, then adapting them to my life, which I am now sharing with you in this book.

In what way are we all a part of this Little Prince?

Before you begin reading this book . . .

Write down all the dreams, desires, and hopes
you had as a child when you were thinking about
your future life.

Be honest and think back to the most sincere
wish you made at the time. Simply remember
what you wanted most for yourself in the past,
even if it seems far-fetched to you today!

_____

_____

_____

_____

_____

_____

_____

_____

"All grown-ups were once children . . . but only a few of them remember it."

—THE AVIATOR

on a cloud

WHEN DID I FIRST READ *The Little Prince*? I don't remember.

Like everyone else, I knew I had read it. But what did I remember about it as time passed by? When did I first understand what it really wanted to tell me? And what lessons did I learn from it in the years that followed?

Oh, to go back to that first time . . .

The time before I grew up. Before I became a rationalist. Before I stepped into the world of grown-ups, the world that I was told was reality. The first time . . . before I forgot.

"Once upon a time, there was the Little Prince." Even if Antoine de Saint-Exupéry never wanted to begin the book with those words, to add "Once upon a time" to the story is to give it back some of its magic, and to give back some of the dreams that we all had as children. And to still believe that magic really exists.

The Little Prince is much more than just a book—it is a worldwide phenomenon, having been translated into three hundred languages and dialects. Yet setting its success aside, the story of the Little Prince remains a part of us. It is a story that began during our childhood and continues to take shape over the years. The Little Prince is a part of ourselves that we have sometimes decided to push back as far as possible from our existence as time passed by, in order to follow the path of adulthood with great strides wherever the opportunity arose. This path, the road to becoming an adult, becomes more and more difficult to deviate from as we grow up.

In the beginning, as we took our first steps in childhood, the path ahead was lined with trees, flowers, birds, and fields. Then, as we grew older and moved forward on this path, small walls began to line the edges, then farther on down the road, a few hedges grew taller and taller.

This path toward adulthood had to be followed. It became impossible to turn around, impossible to deviate from it, impossible to turn back at any moment. We had to continue straight on ahead.

Soon, a few barriers and fences made of wood began to sprout up at the edge of the road; then the first walls were built, stone after stone, covered with ivy, then brick after brick, higher and higher. So high, that after a certain hour the sun was blocked from shining down on us to warm us up. And as the walls rose, shadows formed, growing bigger and bigger, projected against the façades.

The more we continued to move forward, without any other choice, the more we moved away from the stories and the magic that defined our childhood world. Everything became conventional, calculated, Cartesian, logical, concrete, palpable, and demonstrable. Everything had to make sense on paper, with boxes that needed to be checked off. Saint Thomas's philosophy of believing only what he could see with his own eyes began to take pride of place as we entered adulthood. The magic was over.

This approach is the exact opposite of the world of the Little Prince, one that we all experienced when we were younger and invented stories and imaginary scenarios filled with monsters, gods, kings, queens, and continents to conquer, so that our childhood world became more beautiful every day, growing bigger and brighter before our eyes.

Today, *The Little Prince* remains a trace of who we were when we were children. The character represents our inner truths, before time passed by. *The Little Prince* also remains a philosopher's stone capable of speaking to the child we were yesterday. A philosopher's stone capable of transforming our view of the world, and of life, if we so choose. A magical stone that acts on our thoughts in order to transform these high gray walls tightening along the path of adult life into lace made of golden threads, so that once again the light passes through them, so that on each golden scroll, the sun's light and its warmth illuminate our world. As we continue down this path of life, it warms us for the remaining years to come.

After all, gold isn't meant to remain locked up in a chest hidden forever—it should be cultivated and harvested. *The Little Prince* is still here today so that none of us can forget the golden lessons he represents.

Are we capable of rediscovering the child who still lies in each one of us? If so, how can we do this?

What if the Little Prince were to open his inner travel diary to you . . . so that you could get back on the road and rediscover your childhood outlook in a world that sometimes goes a bit mad?

And my Little Prince told me . . .

**You have to have a huge ego to
know how to remain a child . . .
or simply to love yourself.**

HOW TO

look at the world differently

LIKE THE LITTLE PRINCE

ONCE, WHEN I WAS YOUNG, I was playing with the other kids in the square of the town hall of my village of Beynost in the southeast of France. The parish priest called for us to go into the rectory for our catechism lesson. After we had gone through the Old and New Testaments for the umpteenth time, the bell marking the end of the class rang, and all of my friends began to leave. Like any child, I was asking myself a thousand questions about what we had just learned. One of them particularly bothered me.

I pretended to put my things away, then turned to the priest and asked him, "If God created everything, did he create the whole world?"

"Yes," the priest answered.

"And the whole universe too?"

"Yes," the priest answered.

"But . . . after the universe . . . what is there?" I asked him.

He hesitated, then stayed silent. Today I am still waiting for an answer to this question.

Learning how to live like the Little Prince is learning to change the way we look at the world and at the people and the things around us.

Learning how to live like the Little Prince is accepting that everything we have learned while growing up is at best only half true, if not completely false.

We humans all have the same fault: We believe that as we age, we grow as much in spirit as in size. This may be true for the concepts and knowledge we create and learn as human beings, but it is false in terms of our understanding of the world in its entirety. In other words, there is a sensitive, innate knowledge that we tend to lose completely—or at least partly—as we grow older.

As we grow in inches, we think we are also getting closer to the height of knowledge, the sky and the stars of wisdom, when in reality, we are only moving farther away from Earth without actually reaching them. This is one of the key messages of *The Little Prince*: As we grow up, the wisdom and knowledge we think we are amassing cannot replace the magic of the world as perceived by a child—an ability that now eludes us.

Just like in *The Little Prince*, most children see only good or bad, black or white, laughter or tears. Later on, everything lends itself to doubts, confusion, and compromise. Everything in the adult world becomes a palette of shades of gray. We get used to some things, more or less used to other things, and so on.

Is it so enviable to no longer know what is right and what is wrong? To be able to explain, rationalize, excuse, understand, and tolerate everything, even the worst things? There are necessary and acceptable nuances within our lives, whether they are personal, political, amorous, professional, or ecological, that often have colors that blend into each other. It is no longer a question of seeing grayish tones around the edges of our path in life; instead we see a greenish brown adorning the colors of our world. It is the color of decay and mold, where mushrooms start to grow on what were once sincere feelings and honest convictions. It is the color of indecision and inertia, the color of adults who, instead of inquiring and probing, prefer to stick their heads in the sand and live in denial.

Then there are no more roses, no more sunsets; there is no more clear water in the middle of the desert like in *The Little Prince*, because the flowers have withered, huge gray clouds have gathered to block the sun, and the water has stagnated.

But, what if . . .

What if we made the effort to look at the world again through the eyes of the Little Prince?

What would we see? What would come out of it?

Perhaps we are afraid to take a closer look at the lives we have built through the eyes of a child. Perhaps we are afraid we will see the fleeting nature and uselessness of what we have accumulated, what we have bought, what we have fought for, and perhaps we will see that we did these things at the expense of what was really important to us in another time, though not so long ago.

It is so easy to take refuge in the status of being an adult, of *knowing*, of being experienced, in order to avoid putting on our childhood glasses and remembering the dreams we had and the people who once really mattered to us.

It is so easy to convince ourselves that we *know*, when we have gone so far that we have forgotten what truly builds happiness in the eyes of a child.

What if . . .

What if we dared, just for a moment, to turn around and look back at the path we have traveled with that same giggling gaze we once had?

Perhaps the burden is not so terrible, and the mistakes we made are actually not so important.

If we can look at our pasts through the eyes of a child, doesn't the future look more promising? Wouldn't it be great to be able to make choices with our hearts in a simpler way?

If you have children, do an easy test: Tell them an anecdote from your life, a moment when you had to make an important decision, a job change or a big move for example. Then ask them what they would have done in your place. Chances are that your child will start weighing the pros and cons by asking you a few simple questions. Questions that will be based solely on how this choice will affect personal happiness, without any other element or argument having any bearing. It is very likely that your child will ask you questions that you did not ask yourself when deciding, because the questions seem so simple. The obvious is sometimes even more obvious when it comes from the mouth of a child.

Rational, thoughtful, mature decisions are not always the right decisions, because they deliberately remove feelings and sensitivity from the equation, the curvy path of the soul specific to each person, which only the eyes of a child can perceive.

TRAVEL DIARY

So, put on your childhood glasses again to observe the world, understand, and make the right choices.

And my Little Prince told me . . .

We are all beginners,
apprentices in life.
The one who thinks they
are no longer a beginner
becomes one.

be determined and resolute

LIKE THE LITTLE PRINCE

WITH STUBBORNNESS AND TENACITY, the Little Prince never stops trying when at first he doesn't get what he wants, like the drawing of a sheep, or an answer to a question. He insists until he gets it. He never gives up, no matter what the subject, as we see in his interactions with the businessman. When the businessman is too busy to answer his question—"Five hundred and one million what?"—the Little Prince stubbornly asks again until he has his answer.

Even if he may not like all the answers, or if they leave him perplexed or appear to be useless, now he knows them. He may or may not take the answers into account, but one thing is certain: He will continue on his way once he gets what he wants.

Beyond curiosity, it is a sort of quest. And the Little Prince does not intend to abandon his desires or his need for answers until he achieves his quest.

He is determined to know, determined to understand, determined to get what he wants. In his steadfastness, the Little Prince shows us how he takes action, namely by resolving to stay determined until he gets what he wants, a practice that we can all adopt.

It sounds simple. But is it enough to simply insist on getting what you want? Think about it . . .

Yes, sometimes it is as simple as that.

If you know exactly what you want, that is.

Listen to the Little Prince:

"Draw me a sheep please."

So then I made a drawing.

He looked at it carefully, then he said:

"No. This sheep is already very ill. Make me another."

So I made another drawing.

My friend smiled gently at me.

"You have to see it too," he said. "This is not a sheep. This is a ram. It has horns."

So then I did another drawing.

But it was rejected too, just like the others.

"This one is too old. I want a sheep that will live a long time."

Then, for lack of patience, because I was in a hurry to start repairing my engine, I quickly drew this drawing.

And I said, "That's a box. The sheep you want is inside."
I was very surprised to see the face of my young judge get
lighter. "That's exactly how I wanted it!"

In this passage, the Little Prince not only wants a sheep drawn for him, but he also knows exactly what sheep he wants. The aviator has to start again as many times as necessary to get as close as possible to what the Little Prince has imagined. At that moment, a strange phenomenon occurred—while he was very worried, and busy wondering how he could repair his plane to leave again, the aviator submitted to the will of this little blond child who knew exactly what he wanted.

He wanted the sheep so that he could take it back to his planet.

He asked with all his strength that his dream be fulfilled according to his imagination, not according to what is actually possible in the real world.

Do we really know what we want, like the Little Prince? Exactly what we want? Like when we were children? Like when we would write our Christmas wish list? Are we able to be as precise in our desires as the Little Prince is and refuse to be satisfied with anything less?

The simplicity of his childish request actually reveals a real power: a strength within that pays no attention to time. It is a quiet force, never aggressive, yet unflappable in its will, its convictions, and its determination to ask for what we want over and over again. It is a force that has all the time in the world. A force to which we must submit so it doesn't cause us to suffer.

The parents reading this know what I am talking about, when they think back to situations when their children were so stubborn that they just had to relent.

There is no need to get angry or upset; all you need to do is remain firm in what you want, without changing your mind. It is a great lesson for us when the Little Prince points out how sometimes we tell ourselves to move on as quickly as possible with a simple "Oh, it will be fine that way." But can we be satisfied with the results, with what we get, when what we are asking for isn't completely clear? And when we don't stick to what we truly want?

Wouldn't it just be easier to be as determined as the Little Prince in everything we do in order to move our projects forward as quickly as possible, and to progress in our lives? It is simple . . . so simple . . . almost childish . . . to insist so firmly that, without deviating even for a second from our goal, we finally end up reaching it.

TRAVEL DIARY

Be determined; never deviate from
your desires, from your path.

And my Little Prince told me . . .

When you don't come from anywhere, all hopes are allowed.

HOW TO

escape from reality

LIKE THE LITTLE PRINCE

THE LITTLE PRINCE DOES NOT BELONG to the world of the aviator—he comes from another planet entirely. Therefore, he can disregard the rules that govern that world. He has the ability to remove himself from the reality that surrounds him.

Do you remember the imaginary worlds that all of us, as children, were able to create, with castles, cars, dolls, cardboard boxes, and simple bits of string? Like other children, I built many worlds stone by stone when I played with my sister. These worlds functioned according to our own desires and rules—rules that we never hesitated to question for the sake of the story that we wanted to tell, a story that came to life before our very eyes. Our power of imagination back then was limitless. Nothing was forbidden, everything was possible, and we were the only ones dictating the rules of these worlds that felt so real to us at the time.

We have all experienced the feeling of power that came with those moments. We were masters of the universe, much more so than we are today, if we really think about it. We were all like the Little Prince, capable of removing ourselves from reality and its limitations.

But what if we became as imaginative and creative as the Little Prince? Have you sometimes thought that the worlds we created as children really *did* become reality? They existed with such force in the moment—not visible to the eye but present in some form. Didn't they become part of another reality? We have all heard of parallel universes and wormholes. So what if, in all sincerity, at the very same moment we introduced the prince to the princess and our army succeeded in freeing the world from the forces of evil, all this was actually happening somewhere else in the real world?

The Little Prince's strength is that he sees this possibility as a reality. He has the same ability that we had as children; namely, to be able to remove ourselves from the world around us in order to create a better one that reflects our strongest desires. What has happened to this creative superpower that we so easily developed when we were young? This power that allowed us to bend space and time, to change the path of the world and of our own lives?

I, for one, see a simple difference in semantics. The power that we had in the past and the consequences that ensued in the imaginary world of our childhoods are translated today to a concept we call "the power of projection." What if, when we were children, we were capable of projecting ourselves into the life of our dreams? If we just jump back into it, this vision can change the course of reality and bend it to the whims of our desires in order to create a new reality that mirrors the life we want for ourselves.

To be able to escape the world like the Little Prince is to be able to create another one tailored for us. Nothing is fixed in the continuum of life; everything is simply desires, dreams, and inflections that we learn how to project so that, eventually, the most beautiful images from our imagination become part of a real life that we are living.

TRAVEL DIARY

Knowing how to escape
from the world means knowing
how to build your own.

And my Little Prince told me . . .

Be an angel . . .

just to know how to fly.

know the difference between what is urgent and what is important

LIKE THE LITTLE PRINCE

"PROCRASTINATION" HAS BECOME FASHIONABLE in recent years, in all areas of our personal and professional lives. In his book, written so many years ago, Antoine de Saint-Exupéry appears to have foreseen this development. Do not put off until tomorrow what can be done today, as the saying goes.

When the Little Prince warns us to guard against the proliferation of baobabs on our little planet, he is referring directly to the idea that we should never neglect to care for what is at the very source of our survival, even if we don't necessarily take pleasure in it.

Equally important is knowing how to tell the difference between what is urgent and what is important. However, this is often easier said than done, isn't it? Can we really implement this idea on a daily basis? The fleeting pleasures and useless things that consume the minutes of our days take up so much space in our lives, and we attach so much importance to them, that it becomes difficult at times to discern what is pleasant, necessary, amusing, vital, or useful to us.

When I was young and would go to the woodworking shop with my father, one of my first tasks was to replace the bags of sawdust and shavings behind the big machines when they were full. Some of the bags were as big as men, certainly bigger than me. I had to wrap my arms around them to carry them outside and store them under the shed. It was a hard and physical job, especially at that age. However, it was an essential task to keep the factory running smoothly. If the bags were full, the machines would go into "safety" mode and no more pieces of wood could be cut or planed.

The *urgent* task at hand was to complete the furniture, bookcases, and kitchen cabinets for the customers so that the company could exist. But the most *important* thing was to ensure that the furniture could be produced, and one of the prerequisites for this was that the machines continued working. My task was only one link in the chain, but this mission was critical to keeping the machines functioning so that the bags could be filled and the carpets kept free of any wood debris. This way, the carpenters and cabinet makers could do their jobs and the installers could set up these little pieces of art at customers' homes.

I belonged in that environment as a child. I was a part of work that was important, though not necessarily urgent. I think of Bernard and Robert, who are no longer with us, but who worked at the factory and liked to throw me into the piles of shavings. I always somehow managed—with great difficulty and a great deal of laughter—to get myself out.

Am I still able today to know the difference between what is urgent and what is important in the things I do every day? I'm not so sure. This is what the Little Prince said to me during my rereading of the book.

"What is the most important thing in order to do what you do? To write every day?" my Little Prince asked me.

"To take care of myself," I replied.

And he said to me: "You mean . . . what you don't always do."

Although I do my best to understand the difference between what is urgent and what is important in my daily life, like many people, I still don't know how to completely listen to the Little Prince's advice.

What about you? What are the most important and urgent things to do in your life? Do you manage to see the difference between them? What are the baobabs in our lives that we need to watch over so that they don't invade us? Never forget to take care of the most important things, as the Little Prince reminds us. We must never put off until tomorrow what is vital for ourselves today.

TRAVEL DIARY

Important things allow urgent things to exist. The opposite isn't possible.

And my Little Prince told me . . .

What is most important in
chess is neither the pawns,
nor the pieces, it is the
chessboard.

*"If you can succeed in judging yourself,
you are truly wise."*

—THE KING

HOW TO

take care of yourself

LIKE THE LITTLE PRINCE

WATCHING THE SUNSET, up to forty-three times in the same evening on his planet, the Little Prince knows a lot about what he needs to do in order to make himself happy and stay calm. On his little planet, no one dictates his desires or his pleasures—he is the only one who decides whether or not to move his chair a few yards over to watch the next sunset. There is no dress code, no media or magazine to influence him to do what he feels he needs to do to feel good.

The Little Prince is free to be the judge of what pleases him, and he needs no one and no outside advice to make him smile.

He knows how to have fun with nothing and how to take pleasure in everything. Above all, he knows how to pursue what

42

he loves, in this case the soothing, rejuvenating sunset, which he would like to follow ad infinitum. As the narrator says at the end of the encounter between the Little Prince and the lamplighter: *"What the Little Prince dared not admit was that he most regretted leaving that planet because it was blessed with one thousand four hundred sunsets every twenty-four hours!"*

Do we take care of ourselves often enough in our daily lives? Particularly when everything, from homework to family to jobs, keeps pulling us in all directions until we are torn apart trying to take care of everyone else's needs? When we really stop and take a look at our lives it is obvious that we spend more time suffering than taking care of ourselves. As for thinking about doing something good for ourselves, we often save that for our next vacation, if we even dare to take a vacation that is. At the end of the day, who is stopping us from taking the time to think about ourselves, to do something good for ourselves . . . other than ourselves?

So now, do as I do: Turn off your phone (admit it—you haven't done this in the past six months), look around you, and just listen.

No one knows what you are doing, no one can reach you, no one knows where you are. No one can cut you off from your own little world, from this intimate moment, from yourself. You are alone. You are okay. All you need to do in this moment is fill the time with what you like, whether that is music, a book, a daydream, a recipe, a bit of gardening, or simply any activity that you enjoy. Keep your phone off, just for a moment, to make yourself feel good. Please, no matter what time of day you are reading this, try it. Right now—not later. Try it, then do it again.

Learn how to be good to yourself, just like the Little Prince. Even when all the suns are not shining, even when their light is dimmed. Because knowing how to be good to yourself is not only about seizing the day and enjoying life, it is also about knowing how to heal your wounds. And to help time along so it can heal yesterday's wounds. Just as sunsets can ease the Little Prince's sadness, it is up to us to cultivate in our own lives the things that can soften and heal our bleeding hearts.

Now that you've turned off your phone and the screens that distract your mind, can't you see in the distance, from somewhere deep inside of you, desires that appear furtively, in small snapshots? Could it be that your Little Prince is trying to talk to you? It may be difficult to hear his voice, since he is buried so far away and it has been such a long time since you have communicated with the child you once were. And yet, don't these snapshots represent some unfulfilled desires, some pleasures of the moment that have returned to tenderly whisper in your ear?

Listen . . . your Little Prince only wants the best for you. By nurturing your Little Prince, you take care of yourself.

TRAVEL DIARY

You cannot give someone else
happiness if you cannot first
give it to yourself.

And my Little Prince told me . . .

You never know when

you look at people, nature,

or animals for the last time.

protect your dream

WHEN YOU HAVE A DREAM and believe deeply in this dream, some days are not easy. Having a dream and believing in it profoundly can prove to be quite difficult. Having a dream means paving your own path in life, a path that has just one objective: to be happy. It means staying on this path without getting lost on other roads that do not concern you, without letting other people influence you or lead you in another direction, however benevolent their intentions may be, toward a life that is not meant for you.

And it may just so happen that, while you're on this journey, while you're following your star, people threaten your dream, whether deliberately or not. They may criticize you, mock you, stifle you, or attack you. You must find a way to ignore them, to let them slip away as if on a swan's feathers.

Nothing must ever make us doubt our dreams and cause us to deviate from the paths we have chosen. Just like if a sheep were to eat the Little Prince's beloved rose, if the light of our dream is dimmed, all the stars go dark with it. Our dream is a treasure we hold throughout our lives, like the secret chest from our childhood where we once gathered all the treasures so dear to us. This chest that we used to hide in an attic or in our room so that no one would find it and take it away from us. This chest from our childhood was everything to us, and we knew how to protect it.

Our dream becomes our most prized possession as we navigate the calculated and encrypted maze of the adult world, winding through all its obligations and rules. Because, like the chest from our childhood, our dream is priceless.

We all have a dream, even if we don't always believe it will come true. Yet we must keep faith in it. To prevent this dream from being damaged or destroyed we must remember to always protect it. This is how our dreams bloom deep within our souls and, in the end, become reality.

Even if you are the only one who envisions, feels, and understands just how important your dream is, it doesn't matter, because your dream is only about you, only about *your* happiness. It is your quest, your life.

If it remains your lodestar for years, shepherding you closely, there is no doubt that it will eventually become the keystone of a life of happiness that you will have created for yourself. Only you can understand it. Only you know.

Never let anyone trample on your dream, and be careful to always keep it at a safe distance from negative words, negative light, and negative thoughts.

You can also toy with the idea of turning some of your childhood dreams into reality today. I sincerely invite you to do so. At the beginning of this book, there is a section called "Before you start this book" where I asked you to write down all your dreams from your childhood, even the wildest, most extravagant ones. Now I suggest that you take a moment to go back to that list and add some of the childhood dreams that you are starting to remember now. Immersing ourselves in the company of the Little Prince sometimes helps us remember what we have long kept buried.

Finally, why not turn this list into an action plan for future joy? Why not, for example, set yourself the goal of achieving one of the dreams on this list every year? Just for the fun of it, just to thrill the Little Prince inside of you every year.

Dream, pursue your dream, then give it life and anchor it in reality.

Similarly, make sure you never destroy someone else's dream or mock their dream, because you never know what is driving the dream they are choosing to share with you. You must preserve and protect your dream, for yourself and for other people, and nurture it over time.

Protect your dream as if it were your own child. It alone is the living proof that deep inside you, the Little Prince that you once were still exists, and that he is only waiting to reveal himself to the world.

TRAVEL DIARY

When children have a dream, they
make a wish, and that wish comes true.

And my Little Prince told me . . .

Often when someone travels far away, they face their future head-on, rather than simply accepting their fate.

"But the eyes are blind. One must look with the heart."

—THE LITTLE PRINCE

HOW TO

love

LIKE THE LITTLE PRINCE

STRANGELY ENOUGH, AS WE HAVE ALL EXPERIENCED in our own love stories, what might appear as something as natural and simple as the feeling of love is never a given in life. We often have to grasp at it on the fly, without ever truly understanding how it works. As the Little Prince reminds us, love is something we learn.

I recall a very touching wedding ceremony I attended as a child. At the wedding, after the exchange of vows, the couple kissed. At that moment, in my child's mind, I froze and asked myself: "How am I going to do that when I am older? How could I possibly kiss my lover in public in front of everyone? I'll never be able to do that." I was obsessed with this thought for a long time.

It was just a childish fear that I could never share with anyone. It would take many years before I would be able to exchange a simple kiss in front of other people, to completely tune out the time and the place and forget the eyes of others possibly watching. This is also what it means to love: in the heat of the moment, to feel a sensation of being completely alone in the world with the other person.

Most of us have experienced different kinds of love stories and different forms of love. From torrid passion so scorching it becomes destructive to the tranquil comfort of soothing feelings. From loving someone from afar and fantasizing about them to that fusion of hearts where we lose a little bit of ourselves. There are so many different kinds of love stories! All of these love stories have one thing in common: They help us learn more about ourselves and about the other person amid a tumult of feelings that we can neither contain nor channel. We learn who we truly are when we meet this person, who often comes into our life without any warning, at a time when we are ready for it . . . or not. Looking back on each love story, we later ask: Was it the right time? Why did everything go so smoothly? Or on the contrary, why was everything so complicated and heartbreaking?

Whether the love story went well or not so well, we learned more about ourselves the moment this other person came into our lives. We thought we knew who we were, we thought we knew how to react . . . and yet, nothing turned out the way we had imagined it would when we were younger.

In each love story, we also had to experience learning about another person, a stranger, a foreigner, whom we once fantasized about in the most secret recesses of our heart. A person who may not have perfectly fit the image we had formed of them. We thought we knew the person who was made for us, but whether the story went well or not, we often discover and say to ourselves, "At least now I know what I *don't* want anymore."

Loving is a long apprenticeship. It is a gift from heaven that we have to work to unwrap.

"*I was too young to know how to love her,*" the Little Prince says of his rose, because the great strength of a child in the face of love is to know how to question his or her own mistakes, to know how to ask for forgiveness, whereas often, in adulthood, we tend to blame the other person when a love story ends in disaster.

There is so much to learn about love: how to give, how to listen, how to surprise someone and be surprised, how to remain sincere, how to be patient. But a love story will never be as it was in that first moment you met. It won't stay the same, frozen in time. It will evolve depending on the life experiences you have, your own evolution. Over time, these changes will either bring two people together or pull them apart.

To love someone in the same way you did the first moment you met is already to know how to love. Learning to truly love requires just a little bit of extra time, listening, humility, forgiveness, and patience . . . The same patience that children know how to show when they have their first stolen kiss. Do you remember your first kiss?

TRAVEL DIARY

Learning how to love is
the most beautiful journey.

And my Little Prince told me . . .

For her,

I was just a secret garden;

for me,

she was my whole life.

turn the page

LIKE THE LITTLE PRINCE

TAKING FLIGHT AND LEAVING THE PAST behind is not so simple, because over time we develop habits that become ways of life— they are how our world, and its balance, are built. When we are forced to change, either by necessity or by desire, it is not easy to start over again, to turn the page, especially on a chapter that has been fostered and constructed over several years.

In the distant past, our ancestors did not undergo so many drastic life changes. Their lives were mapped out, from child-hood to marriage, from parenting to death. If someone was born the child of a peasant, it was impossible to abandon that life and lead a completely different one. For better or worse, everything was planned, making it impossible to escape. Starting over was rare in a world where everyone conformed to expectations, whatever their social status, culture, or country. Thus, the history of human beings continued, from generation to generation, condemned to repeat the same story over and over again. Individuals, couples, and society as a whole observed the same traditions, made the same mistakes, preached the same beliefs, taught the same truths, and experienced the same dynamics. For a long time, the world has continued to function on this loop. Only a few curious people, explorers, inventors, and researchers have tried to push the limits of knowledge, often at the cost of their reputations, their memberships in different groups, or even their lives.

Today, this repetitive system, this straitjacket of life in which everyone is trapped regardless of their status, this life with no way out, is over. Freedom has become a given for many. The freedom to stay, to change, to leave, the freedom to start over and over again . . . and what a freedom it is!

Yet what a burden it is, this freedom that has been bequeathed to us. Despite the past's compartmentalization of choices and opportunities, it was much easier to let oneself be carried along by life yesterday than it is to choose today. We only experience envy when we know there's something other than what we have. When we don't know, we want only what we're told life should be. And the rules we're told to follow don't make us unhappy because we don't know any others.

Today, everything is known, everything is visible, everything is conceivable—or at least it seems so—and everything appears possible. We can change from this moment forward, decide to leave for another life more compatible with our true selves, a life that seduces us. The world has become a buffet—full of places to visit, jobs to discover, opportunities, encounters, pleasures, and people to love.

The only thing left to do is the most complicated thing of all: choosing. Choosing to take the first step, to turn the page and change our habits or our lives. Because leaving something behind, according to the Little Prince, means knowing what you are leaving behind. It means telling yourself, a few days before moving, before changing jobs, or before changing your life: "This is the last time that . . ."

Turning the page is not easy, but today, unlike yesterday, it is possible. It is often only our fears that prevent us from starting over, when almost all the obstacles have been removed. But our fears are fierce. If there is one person who can help us take the necessary step to turn the page, it is the child we once were. That Little Prince, sitting wisely on his planet, dreaming of endless possibilities, of faraway places, and of traveling the world, just as we once did. This Little Prince, whom we leave completely immobile and lifeless when we don't listen to what makes him tick—what drives us.

Do we have to wait until the last day of our lives to have regrets? How can we leave our friend, the child we once were, to die of boredom? How can we fail to take the first step to write a new page of our life? Go ahead, take that step!

Turning the page
is continuing to write the story
of your life over and over again.

And my Little Prince told me . . .

**It is always on the last day
that we finally know what we
should keep, what we have
earned, and what we need to
leave behind.**

"And what good does it do you to own the stars?"

—THE LITTLE PRINCE

be rebellious and incorruptible

LIKE THE LITTLE PRINCE

THE LITTLE PRINCE DOES NOT SUBMIT to any power. While visiting an asteroid inhabited by a single king, even as he is commanded to stay to be the Minster of Justice, he takes his leave. The Little Prince is rebellious, incorruptible, and cannot conceive of this pseudo-authority that would allow any monarch to have complete control over him, over what he should do and think, let alone a king who does not reign over anything in particular.

To remain insubordinate in adulthood, to live without compromising our beliefs and what we say . . . what a challenge! One that is quite difficult at times, can we all agree?

And yet, even if certain arrangements are necessary for the good of the community, must we submit to any form of power that presents itself? Must we submit to it against our will and our better judgment? Whether this power is of a legal, hierarchical, governmental, religious, patriarchal, or political nature, in reality it represents only the law of the strongest. The law of the strongest is not a law that we must accept in all circumstances. Constantly bending to the will of others only leads to becoming a hunchback long before the end of our lives.

Once, when I was very young, my grandmother reprimanded me for the umpteenth mistake I had made. She pointed at me with an accusing finger, aimed at the medallion I wore around my neck, warning me: "Be careful, Jesus can see you!" This individual, depicted on my baptism medallion, had absolute power and could decide to punish me whenever he wanted. Unless, that is . . .

I took my medallion between my fingers at the end of the long chain, looked at it, looked at my grandmother, who seemed so old to me at the time, and quickly hid the medallion behind my back and responded: "Well, look, now he can't see me anymore!" Then I went back to my business with a smile while my grandmother burst out laughing.

It is so easy, and so obvious, to free oneself from the powers that be when we are young, as was the case in my story. Later on, however, religion sometimes persuades us to blame ourselves, or it makes us feel guilty in a way that forces us into submission.

Everyone is free to believe what they believe. Religious faith is not the point of the story, just an illustration of how power can become tyrannical, and how we can choose at any moment not to be subjected to it anymore, but instead to simply live with it, as equals, or not.

It is so easy to let our fears constrain us, fears that grow as we get older. All forms of power leverage our fears about life and death against us, and this goes far beyond religion. It is also easy to give up entire parts of our lives, of our freedom, in the face of political pressures and become automatically subservient for no other reason.

Being rebellious like the Little Prince doesn't mean being recalcitrant, fanatical, angry, or vengeful; it means simply believing in ourselves above all, and following our unique paths in life. It means not being afraid, not giving in, and knowing, like him, how to be free to stay or to go.

TRAVEL DIARY

The only things you should
surrender to are your dreams.

And my Little Prince told me . . .

I believe in everything
that eludes people,
and I distrust everything
that comes from them.

remain humble

IN ADULTHOOD, SOMETIMES some people earn a little bit too much money a little bit too often and a little bit too quickly with a little too much pride. This can happen following the discovery of a talent or a newfound success, or, very often, thanks to a boost—or more like a sudden catapulting—into a life of ease that puts their foot in the stirrup of a horse much too high for them.

And there, from the vertiginous heights of this masterly point of view, vanity takes over, and they start thinking they are exceptional and forget the true meaning of this success. Vanity prevails when we forget the reasons that propelled us to the top and choose not to focus on our talent or our knowledge but instead on our greatness!

Working hard to achieve success rarely leads to vanity but often to humility, when the paths taken have been so narrow and the hills so difficult to climb. When you do what you can, everything you can, you become exhausted, it's true, but you never become vain.

Someone told me a few years ago: "When things start to work for you, you will become like everyone else, your head will get too big!" I don't know if he was talking about himself or me at the time. I answered him with derision: "When you succeed, if you get too big for your britches, your head needs to swell up at the same time to keep you balanced."

And those first days came, when the seeds I had planted and nurtured for so many years began to germinate, then to grow slowly, without any vanity involved. Because as I enjoyed this first meager harvest, I humbly observed and studied those who, whatever their field, had realized their dream after working hard. Strangely enough, athletes, writers, inventors, musicians, engineers, designers, and actors that I have seen reach a high level of success were far from vain. They all shared a desire to continue doing, building, and achieving.

I heard less and less from this person, who said he was "happy for me." No matter how many times I tried to call him, he responded less and less. Eventually, this person slowly eliminated me from his circle of friends. The problem, I later realized, was that he was projecting his own personal issues onto me. The "big head" he attributed to me was really just a reflection of his own personality.

One can also become vain through projection or through jealousy.

Strangely enough, vanity can emerge in some children as early as their first days in school, and for the same reasons as an adult who has been given too much without having had to give much in return.

On the playground, Thomas was one of those people. He came from a wealthy family and he was always showing off the latest gifts he had received, sometimes for a good grade, sometimes for his birthday, and often for no reason at all. He always had the nicest clothes, the coolest backpack, or the latest gadget—and rarely because he had earned them.

By constantly boasting, by crushing us with his wealth, by showing us pictures of the wonderful vacations he enjoyed at the other end of the world, and while sneering at the motor homes or trailer parks of others, Thomas ended up like any other conceited person. That is, once the magic of the show was over, he found himself alone or almost alone in the schoolyard.

Just like on the planet visited by the Little Prince, the vain man remains alone in his mirror.

Vanity borders on solitude. Only humility commands the admiration and respect of other people for work done and projects accomplished. Look at today's celebrities, who parade across our television sets, having nothing to sell but their own images. They are simply shooting stars who epitomize the fleeting nature of fame and fortune. No one is fooled by the vanity, shallowness, and emptiness with which they puff themselves up. Just like the child in us, the Little Prince does not allow himself to be impressed or duped by the Conceited Man.

As for humility, if we spend every day cultivating it in what we do and in who we are, it blossoms into a beautiful soul, a person to whom everyone wants to get closer.

TRAVEL DIARY

Remain humble, and
you will become great.

And my Little Prince told me . . .

It is when you think

you are somebody

that you become nobody.

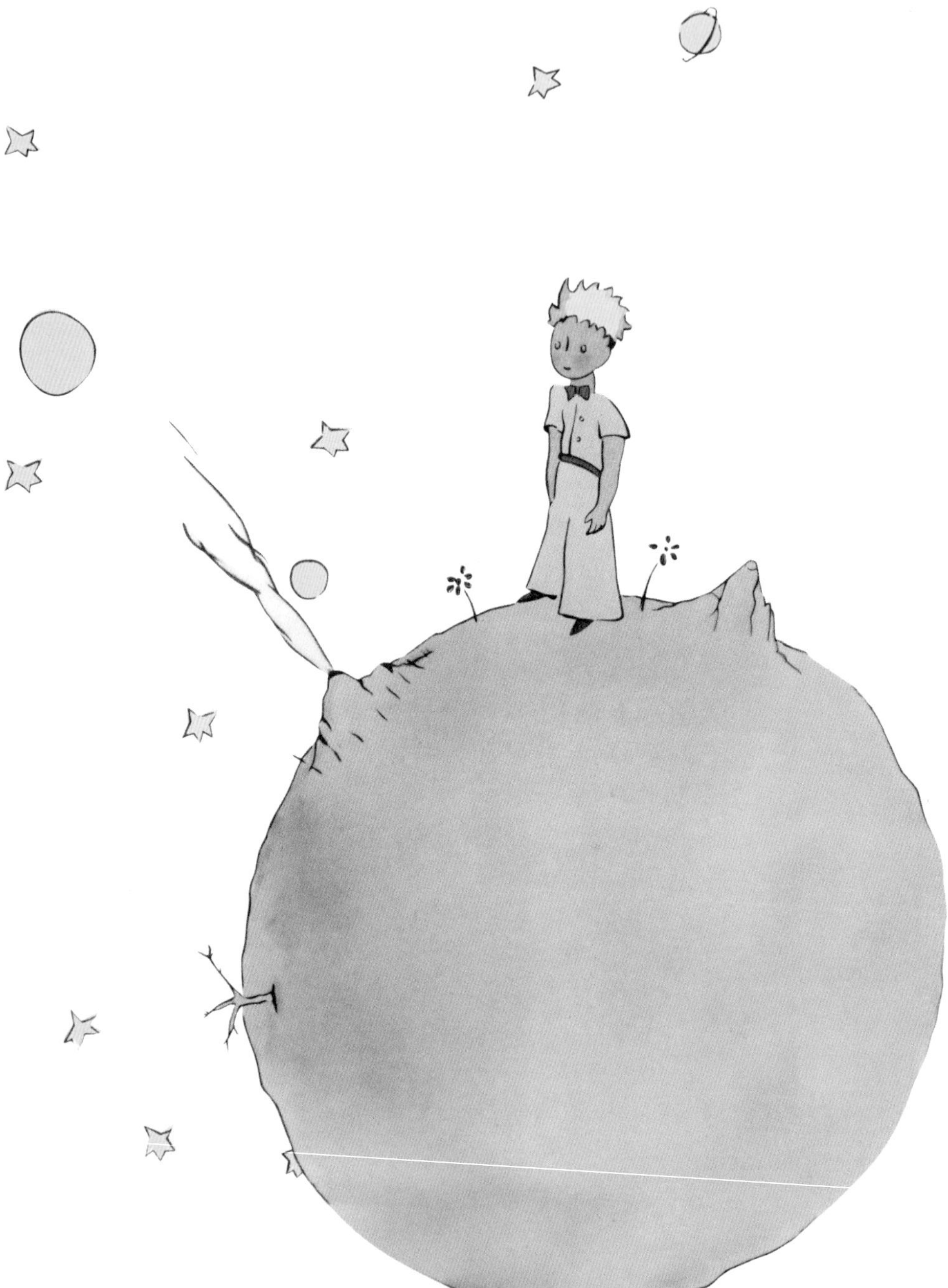

HOW TO

stay curious, adventurous, and awed by everything

LIKE THE LITTLE PRINCE

WE CAN DISCOVER THE WORLD and its riches only by ourselves, whether these treasures are ephemeral or essential. When I think back to my childhood, I had one thing in common with other people, with other children, with you—namely, the desire to know more, to discover, to touch things, to test things out. In short: curiosity. Just like the Little Prince, who is constantly seeking knowledge with his endless questions:

> —If a sheep eats little bushes, does it eat flowers too?
> —A sheep eats anything it finds in its reach.
> —Even flowers that have thorns?

—Yes, even flowers that have thorns.

—Then the thorns, what use are they?

Are we all still as curious about the world around us today as we were when we were young?

The obligations of our daily life, work, friends, family, and professional circles now take up such a big part of our lives. Do we still have time to be curious and carefree in our everyday lives? Do we still make the time to discover, take an interest in, and perhaps even marvel at a fact, a word, a smell, a color, or a new texture? Our time-consuming habits are so pervasive they fill up every hour of our day, even if we have optimized our schedules and our time. We have done so only to squeeze in yet another new habit, or a new constraint, or a new repetitive task without leaving any room for a simple moment of reverie or curiosity.

The clouds continue to float over our heads, but we no longer see them. Every night, the bees return to their hives when the sun sets. And we find it normal that the Earth continues its infinite dance among the stars without a hiccup, in spite of what mankind has done to it. Everything is normal and accepted— nothing seems exceptional to us anymore—and yet, each new day that makes the petals of flowers open, and the dew fall on leaves with infinite finesse, is actually quite spectacular and magical. What if, just for a second, we could take the time to drink our coffee with our noses pressed against the window, watching this marvel of a world, which is reborn every day, rather than hypnotizing ourselves in front of a television screen?

Oh, the television. This little box that often offers only the most hideous face of the world, or the consequences of what human beings have made of it. Yet it is so easy to simply open the blinds and push the windows wide open. Even if the scene is not perfect, and even if, of course, we cannot compare the sight of an infinite azure horizon of a mountain range stretching as far as the eye can see with that of a concrete city. Yet, in spite of everything, this is the gift that the world offers us every day, because for each of us, the sun has risen.

The Little Prince knows how to look at every sunset. On his little planet, by just moving his chair over a little, he manages to see forty-three of them in just one day. So how can we, like him, know how to recognize the beauty of the world without needing to annotate it, freeze it, or explain it? How can we learn to simply enjoy it and bathe in its beauty as soon as possible? Are we capable of this one small thing? Are we still able to smile at this Little Prince sleeping in the depths of our subconscious? Are we capable of taking his hand, not to lead him but to let him guide us into the future . . . ?

"Sunshine color" is what I called the color yellow when I was a child. This made the teacher smile, and she told my parents about this strange moniker. Sunshine color. I could not deny it. It was impossible to convince myself otherwise. Even today, these words echo in my ears. To me, the color yellow still does not exist. "Look for your sun, look for your sunshine color," my Little Prince kept telling me. As I write this, I am sitting by the sea, some forty years later. And just ke yesterday, yellow does not exist here, it is only the "sunshine color"—it was yesterday's paths that have finally led me here and now.

TRAVEL DIARY

The world lights up when you know how to look at it.

And my Little Prince told me . . .

The things I like best are the ones that have no reason to exist.

be rich in what you have

IS IT BETTER TO BE RICH in what we have, or to be rich in what we own?

It seems easy to answer the question from the point of view of an enlightened adult, arguing from a philosophical point of view that "What we own ends up owning us," or that "Inner wealth is the only wealth that counts," and ending by concluding that "One who is satisfied with little is rich in everything . . ." These are all beautiful ideas that we often hear, learn, and relay to others. But in reality, do we truly *live* them, do we apply them in our everyday lives? Are they even conceivable when it comes to human nature?

I do not intend to reignite this debate, which has long agitated thinkers, philosophers, and spiritual leaders alike—I am interested only in the Little Prince's approach to this notion. What matters here is the way in which we as children judged this idea of wealth. Do you remember your childhood treasures? Do you remember the bag of marbles you used to try to fill up during recess at school? Do you remember bartering on the playground or trading toys?

As children, we liked to accumulate things, but there is a major difference between what we do when we are young and what we do as the adults we later become. Children only amass and collect wealth that is, or seems, useful to them, not to the world. Like adults, children are sometimes jealous of what they see in their peers that they do not have. But in the end, most of the time, after some reflection, this envy passes quickly. With the exception of certain repeated caprices, children like what they have and are largely satisfied with it most of the time. These riches are chosen, cultivated, and accumulated based on what they want, not because of any "duty" to own them.

"It is useful to my volcanoes, and it is useful to my flower, that I own them," the Little Prince explains. This is how he feels, how he understands this experience. That is why these "riches" make him happy, because they are useful to him just as he is useful to them, in his eyes.

Weren't you content with what you had when you were young? Even with something small? Often yes, because this "wealth" was enough to make you happy. In this sense, you were rich, because what you had contributed to your happiness.

As children, we were rich in what we had, because we were rich in what we loved.

What would have been the point for us to constantly accumulate things that would not have contributed to our happiness or to our pleasure? That is, however, strangely enough, exactly what many of us chose to do later in life. We started to accumulate things in order to "prove to" or "follow the new trend of." In short, we acquired everything that society commanded us to in order to stay up to date and fashionable, molding to the standards of our time. Riches as ephemeral as they were insubstantial, when not one of them fulfilled our most sincere desires like the little treasures that we cuddled under our pillows as children.

But what if . . . ?

Once again, I'd like to take a look at the possibilities the Little Prince inside of us has in mind.

What if . . .

. . . What if we emptied our closets and piled everything we owned on a giant table? What would we keep? Honestly? How many of these objects would really contribute to our happiness? How many of them would be useful for our enjoyment of life? This exercise is easier when you move from one home to another, as I experienced a few months ago. By the time I finished packing, I had filled many more garbage bags than travel bags for the new beginning ahead of me.

Like children evaluating their riches after trick-or-treating, we can keep only what we like at the time—that's all.

Should we, like the Little Prince, list all the reasons that we like something? The reasons why we keep each object close to us? If our possessions do not contribute to our happiness, then, in the eyes of a child, they are useless.

TRAVEL DIARY

To be rich in what you have is to be rich in what you love, to end up being rich in what you are.

And my Little Prince told me . . .

The question mark
is a symbol of doubt,
and its drawing,
half a heart.

"You become forever responsible for what you have tamed.
You are responsible for your rose . . ."

—THE FOX

HOW TO

work at what you love and feel useful in what you do

LIKE THE LITTLE PRINCE

WHILE EACH LIFE STORY IS A SAGA that is written chapter by chapter, when we are young, we are not alone in writing the first volumes. From infancy to taking our first steps, our parents, our teachers, and others around us are the ones who "write" our first experiences, our first tastes, our first discoveries.

These first volumes of life pile up and are filled with experiences and knowledge that we do not choose, but toward which we are directed to discover and test. Consequently, the more diverse and rich the knowledge we gain in childhood is, the broader the possibilities are for our future.

Believing that we can choose a profession without having been exposed to different subjects is an illusion. When we don't know any better, we have no choice—we pursue a course of study by default in the few or only fields we have ever known.

As adults, we become the sum of the experiences we were immersed in as children. We go on to practice the profession for which we have been conditioned since the first chapters, the first volumes, of our lives. This is how teachers, doctors, lawyers, sailors, and construction workers are often trained, based on the influence of their families.

And yet, along the way, from childhood to adolescence, we all picked up a pen at some point, disregarding outside influences, to write new chapters of our lives. It is then quite possible that tension and contradictions appeared between the paths we chose to follow and the paths to which we felt drawn. And yet, we continued on our merry way because of our ignorance and our fear of the field we cherished at the time. A lack of confidence, a lack of support, and life itself sometimes lead us into a world or a profession for which, despite appearances, we are not suited.

Have you experienced this situation? Maybe you are living it right now. Maybe you have a certain scope of knowledge, or maybe you're working in a respectable profession, yet you don't always feel like you belong.

So, what should you do? What should you do when you remember the dreams you had, the desires you may have written down in your diary years ago? Secret dreams of art, of grand gourmet tables, of becoming a veterinarian or an architect, of traveling the world. When today, the task at hand is to urgently send tax assessments to your company before the deadline.

Am I in the right place? Do I like what I do? These are questions that, as soon as they appear, never stop coming back, spinning around, dancing before our eyes. These are questions that we know we will have to answer at some point. This can take time—years!—and involves calling everything we've ever known into question. Until now, our lives have been defined by the path we are currently on. Should we wait for a midlife crisis in our forties or fifties, which is so symptomatic of this great turn, to redesign our life? Or perhaps, as quickly as possible, should we instead reread those first pages we wrote as children, filled with joy and playfulness, represented today by the Little Prince inside us? Those pages in which we imagined ourselves doing a job we were passionate about, a job where we felt useful to ourselves and others.

The Little Prince that we embodied then had high esteem for the person they dreamed of being, because that esteem was superimposed in the imagination of the person they were going to become. What if we reconnected with our past dreams, the dreams of the child we once were? Some may think, "They were ridiculous!" Maybe they were ridiculous. Or maybe this is just our way of reassuring ourselves that the path we have chosen is the correct one, and the doubts we are experiencing have no bearing on the future.

Our youthful desires didn't come out of nowhere. They surfaced and we became attached to them. We nurtured them not as daydreams, but as premonitions of our future self and the role we wanted to play in the world, which was opening up before our eyes.

It is never too late to change or to question our lives. Even as we sigh about our lives, and our Little Prince keeps telling us that our happiness lies somewhere else, at the opposite end of the spectrum of how we are currently living and in perfect harmony with those early chapters of our childhood. It is not too late to begin a new chapter.

If you feel this uneasiness in your life, remember that. And ask your Little Prince what your true desires were back then.

Only he knows the answer—that is, if you know how to really listen to him.

TRAVEL DIARY

Reward yourself with the
freedom to do what calls to you now.
Freedom is doing what you love.

And my Little Prince told me . . .

**When someone tells you that
it is impossible, remember that
they are talking about their
limitations, not yours.**

leave your mark on the world

LIKE THE LITTLE PRINCE

THE AVIATOR'S FINAL WORDS of the book still echo in the distance—*"Send me word immediately that he's come back...."*—as he reflects on the desert where he first met the Little Prince, even though in reality, somewhere, the Little Prince never left.

The Little Prince that we carry deep inside of us is always there throughout our lives. We can forget him, he can fall asleep, but he never leaves us. The difficulty lies in accepting this part of the child that we all keep buried. We "see" ourselves growing up, then growing old. Yet through all these years, we only "see" ourselves as we are in the present moment. It is a delicate art to look at ourselves differently and instead accept that the child we once were has never left our sides throughout our lives. It takes great humility for the adults we have become to admit this.

We take such pride in being grown up, in having become so wise, expanding our souls to become adults and relegating the child within us to vague memories. In reality, it was this child with tiny hands who carried us through life to become who we are today.

Ego, ego, I can hear you. A little humility, please, and respect for the greatness of spirit that this child knew how to project in order to create the adult that we have become. We owe this child everything—who we are, what we think, what we still dream of—everything. Without them, who would we be? Think about it: Who would you be?

Throughout our lives, the Little Prince we once were has left a mark on us that defines who we are today, even if it is sometimes difficult to admit it to ourselves, when we think we have built and controlled every part of our lives in a reasonable way.

Leaving a mark on the world, the mark of the open-minded, dreamy, optimistic child we once were, is the ultimate gift that the Little Prince still knows how to give us, when we find ourselves lost in the jungle of our lives, with no way out and no sun shining in. Only the Little Prince within us can enable us to bounce back when life brings us to our knees. It is in this living source, via this mark he has left in the folds of our soul, that we can at any moment be reborn and find hope.

When we look at the fragility of our adult lives, we notice that, with just the slightest change, the entire edifice can collapse. If we are still standing today, we have this Little Prince to thank, who never let us down, even if we didn't always know what to call him.

Yes, it was him who gave you the strength to get up again. Now, what is left as we get older? A growing desire to leave a mark on the world, through our projects, our successes, our children.

Does this desire become pressing when we feel that we are ready to become the Little Prince again, to let him invade our thoughts again? I don't know. But at some point a desire to leave something behind, a part of ourselves, and contribute something to the world, becomes increasingly urgent. Not necessarily for posterity's sake, but so we are not forgotten, to have the feeling of having existed.

To be honest, this desire is quite narcissistic, but then again, why do we write? To leave a mark on the world of course, not for tomorrow but for today. To write for tomorrow is to miss out on the impact our words can have on the present. Instead, I want to leave my mark on the world, through my words, through my relationships, through my books . . . always for others.

Many of the authors I have read over the years have become friends, roommates, allies of my sleepless nights. Many have helped me. Like them, my goal when I first started writing could be summed up as follows: "If I can help at least one person . . . I will have won."

Reading the kind messages of gratitude I receive is a reminder that my Little Prince has given me, thanks to you, a gift that goes far beyond the promise he made to me in fifth grade, when I was writing my first illustrated story, *The Key to Dreams*. In the end, we are not the ones leaving our mark on the world; in the best-case scenario, if we know how to listen to him, it is the Little Prince we once were.

TRAVEL DIARY

We become, and we leave what
we have always been.

And my Little Prince told me . . .

Ego, ego . . . We are all ego.

All ego and all equal.

"Here is my secret. It is very simple: It is only with the heart that you can see rightly. What is essential is invisible to the eye."

—THE FOX

be understood by others

LIKE THE LITTLE PRINCE

IN THE VERY FIRST PAGES of the Antoine de Saint-Exupéry book, the Little Prince appears as the youthful soul of the narrator. With his drawing, he tries to convince the grown-ups around him of the magic that can still be cultivated in our adult lives— lives that have become so Cartesian, so prosaic, and so often devoid of imagination.

Presenting each adult with his illustration of a somewhat long and odd-looking shape, he asks "What do you see?" Unfortunately, the answer is always the same—"It is a hat"—and they fail the test. None of the adults see through the eyes of a child, of imagination, to see what is possible within this frumpy form: a boa constrictor digesting an elephant. He would have liked to share conversations from one Little Prince to another. However, this proves impossible, because his fellow human beings tend to stifle their own personal Little Prince as they get older. The narrator does not condemn this fact; he simply notes how things are, namely this sad state of being an adult and being able to hold only adult discussions.

Have you ever been on the receiving end of attacks from individuals who sneer at your words when you are talking about your dreams? The desires carried by your own personal Little Prince that develop in your imagination and blossom in your daydreams? When you decide to share them with people, even with family and friends, haven't you found yourself put down at times by wing-cutters devoid of imagination and desire? This can be a vexing, hurtful moment that touches us deeply. It is a difficult moment to live through, because here we are, expressing ourselves with an open heart in all sincerity, with unfiltered vulnerability, and our openness is disparaged.

We then become reluctant to repeat the experience, because beyond being misunderstood, the scathing comments leave us with no choice but to justify ourselves, to pass for an enlightened person, or . . . to fall into line with "adult," pretentious thinking. We forget the impetus of our Little Prince, the echo of the voice of our childhood spirit.

However, there is another way. There are several things to learn from this unfortunate experience . . .

Never silence your childlike soul, and always stay in touch with your dreams. Nurture the Little Prince that we all carry within us, to constantly renew yourself, to marvel at the world, and to preserve this refreshing outlook on life. Share the desires of your Little Prince only with people who are as capable as you are of cherishing him over time so as not to be disappointed by any cynical attitudes you may face. I don't mean to judge these killjoys, these people who are too serious, too attached to their own wisdom and their greatness, too harshly. As they grew, they lost touch with the most precious parts of themselves. By turning their back on their Little Prince, they lost their joie de vivre, their joy of living.

I just hope that we can get close enough to them to perhaps convince them, with our smiles and our dreams, to reconnect to their own little voice, to the child buried so deeply inside of them they can no longer hear its sighs.

Never become a person who disparages or crushes someone's dreams, because in doing so you not only condemn the desires and dreams of someone else, but you also destroy the magic that your own Little Prince is giving to you.

We can adapt, but we must never betray the child we carry within ourselves.

TRAVEL DIARY

To make yourself understood by others
is to stay true to yourself.

And my Little Prince told me . . .

**An adult is a wise child and
a child a wise adult.**

"It is something that's been too often neglected. It means, 'to create ties'..."

—THE FOX

HOW TO

connect to others

LIKE THE LITTLE PRINCE

IF THERE IS ONE CONTINUOUS THREAD between childhood and adulthood, it is the feeling of loneliness. This feeling can be felt when physically alone and when surrounded by other people.

Throughout the book, the Little Prince is constantly looking for friends, particularly people he can get along with and people who are just like him. He doesn't find friendship with the drunkard or the businessman, but he continues his quest nonetheless, always looking for a friend, someone with whom he can spend his life.

The fox introduces him to the concept of taming someone, approaching someone little by little to create a bond with each shared moment. It is astonishing to see how quickly children, even when they don't know each other, will begin to interact, warm up to each other, and get to know each other little by little. Everyone has surely seen or experienced a situation where children who have never met before are put in the same room so that they can get to know each other. For example, children who are told to play by themselves after a meal so the adults can catch up with each other or relax. At first, the children are typically very shy with each other, but for only fifteen minutes! And by the end of the day, it is often impossible to separate them. This is the magic of childhood, where there are no rules, no walls, and where children take the first step to "tame" each other in just a few moments.

For adults, however, we have set up so many safeguards, protocols, and social rules to protect ourselves, and to reassure ourselves about the people we have become, that it is much more complicated to put three adult strangers in a room and expect them to connect in a few moments, to share sincerely, to open up to each other without fear, and to laugh together with no false pretenses. In this situation, politeness and small talk are the best you can expect with adults.

It's a pity to have lost the ability to approach someone spontaneously and create a strong bond, something we did with so much ease as children.

So what happened?

How, year after year, did we all get so locked up in our own little worlds, our own little lives, that we refuse to let strangers in unless we've screened them first in order to protect ourselves?

Today many of us—almost all of us—are quite alone in our lives. And yet, the Little Prince never stops knocking on the door of our minds as soon as the opportunity arises, to tell us "Go and talk to her! Go and talk to her, damn it! What are you waiting for?"

Are you afraid? Ashamed? Helpless?

How should we deal with this moment?

It seems that, as we have grown up, we have lost the very essence of what it means to be human, namely the ability to share and connect with others in just a few moments, as we did so easily on the playground as children.

What if, the next time we are invited somewhere or the next time we go to a bar, we try to re-create that childhood experience? That is to say, to remain open to all encounters and all discussions, to talk to strangers and dare to make the first move. Yes, this requires us to go beyond ourselves, to overcome certain fears, often fears that we have created in our own minds. The fear of being rejected, the fear of exposing ourselves, for example. But how can we establish ties and build relationships without taking a risk, without having confidence in the other person as well as in ourselves, to start a new conversation or to spark a new encounter?

Is spontaneously connecting to someone else just for children? Or can we pretend when meeting new people that we are back in that room playing, filled with curiosity, without any judgment or protective armor? We too can all come out laughing, delighted, cheerful, and even crying when we don't want to leave, and hoping to see these new people again. We too can create ties that will become indestructible, just like the ties between the fox and the Little Prince.

TRAVEL DIARY

The bonds we create are the
true meaning of our lives.

And my Little Prince told me . . .

**Each person is the missing
link between the Earth and
the heavens.**

HOW TO

take time to live

LIKE THE LITTLE PRINCE

IDLE, CAREFREE, AND PLAYING GAMES . . . in childhood, time flies when you are having fun and taking all the time you need to do what you love.

Remember when it was time for dinner and you were in your room playing with your toys, in the middle of acting out a scene from an elaborate story you created, and you heard those incessant calls from the kitchen asking you to come to the table and eat? If you had just a few more minutes, you could have finished your scene and your hero could have entered the castle. But the calls kept coming, and you had to obey, yielding to a schedule set by the grown-ups for a meal that could not possibly suffer another minute of waiting.

Taking the time to live is a natural inclination for children. In adulthood, however, after having undergone many forms of conditioning, time becomes a commodity that must be useful, profitable, and productive. All adults then begin to suffer from this version of time they have created, until they become its slaves, before ending up its prisoners.

Isn't it strange, this invention of technology meant to "save time," like, for example, a pill that cuts off thirst? In reality, this invention is no stranger than many others, such as the apps on our smartphones whose only objective, like this pill, is to save time, to save minutes so that they can be filled with other activities.

We rush through life, we zip through our weeks and our calendars, and we fit so many things into each day in a race to hyperproductivity. But what is the point of it all? What is this bingeing really hiding? Why push ourselves so hard if we can't find time to take a moment for ourselves or to spend time with friends? To take time to savor life is a notion that becomes completely foreign to us in adulthood. Even while on vacation— which is the last straw—when we feel we have to fill our days of rest and idleness by traveling to a foreign city, waking up at dawn (don't forget to set the alarm clock!), having lunch on the go while waiting in line in the sun like sheep, just to catch a glimpse of a tiny painting on the ceiling of the Sistine Chapel, in front of which we cannot stop for even a moment because the crowd is shoving us from behind. And after that, let's do even more!

Let's enjoy a walk here, a hike there, before a pottery workshop, a salsa class . . .

Enjoy! We must enjoy! We must absolutely enjoy!

But we can't enjoy life when we zip around without any pleasure at all doing a million activities and filling up our lives, which are already ready to explode.

And then there was the period of confinement during the global pandemic. Do you remember the anxiety and idleness of those first days, when it was impossible to do half the things we did before? We tried to fill this time with cooking, spring cleaning, tidying up, and playing with our children, but after a few days, once all the electrical outlets had been swabbed, and we had overdosed on television, and we had done the rounds of all possible "hobbies," what happened? Some of us became depressed, while others began to read, but somehow, whether the situation was forced on us or not, we had to accept it. To live in confinement as best we could, and without the packed agendas that we had before. We had to accept, again and again, day after day, that we needed to take the time to do each thing calmly and purposefully.

Strangely enough, despite all the disasters that the pandemic and home confinement brought on, these conditions forced us to slow down, and, for some of us, to rediscover our spouses, our children, and our passions that had been left behind for lack of . . . time. We became children again, with a notion of time that depended only on our own pleasure when it came to having our meals or engaging in our activities, without any other obligations.

We took back the power to do what we wanted when we wanted—we simply took back the time to live. Perhaps we should not forget this in the future? Isn't it better, like the Little Prince, to go for a walk to enjoy some fresh water at the fountain, rather than to deprive ourselves of the pleasure of drinking?

And what if, from now on, we keep in mind our confinement, and reflect on it from time to time, so that tomorrow, this tyranny of "productive time" will no longer rule our lives?

TRAVEL DIARY

Time is only what I make of it.

And my Little Prince told me . . .

There is a trap to avoid in life: to live quickly in order to die quickly.

free yourself from the judgment of others

LIKE THE LITTLE PRINCE

"WHY AM I UGLY?" I asked myself this fundamental philosophi-cal question, dangling from the fence in my parents' yard, at the age of just four years old. In the alley below, a group of young people regularly passed by, going I don't know where, to tell me: "You, you're ugly!" and laughing. What cruelty on the part of the older kids on their way to adulthood! I couldn't understand and so, furious, I shook the fence while shouting out to whomever could hear me: "And why am I ugly?"

What arbitrary judgment, this "grown-up" judgment, this incredible stupidity developing at the same speed as their legs were growing. I didn't understand why I was being attacked and judged, when I was just a little kid, when I was just watching the world on the other side of the fence, the world I wanted to be a part of.

I wanted to follow in their footsteps and jump over the fence into their world.

We are all forced to endure the judgment of others, this deformed mirror that follows us from the most tender age of childhood to the hollowed wrinkles of old age. It is impossible to escape. No matter what we say, no matter what we do, these gazes haunt every step that we take outside the drawn lines of life's conventional path, even this simple example from my own childhood, when I had no influence, when I hadn't said a word or done anything, even when I was so little I could barely move my toes.

The judgment of others exists and it reigns supreme—that is, as long as we acknowledge its existence and give it any power. Should we judge others, condemn them, even to death, as the king asks of the Little Prince? What good would that have done him? Earned him a few cents of recognition, secured him a place next to the king, who was king only in the reflection of his own magnificence. What does the Little Prince do then, when the king goes so far as to ask him to judge himself?

In both examples, the Little Prince does the same thing: He ignores the king's power. The power that wanted to force him to stay on this empty planet, the power that wanted to corrupt him, the power that offered him a place by judging someone else, the power that went so far as to want to force him to question himself, to judge himself, right here, on this tiny planet.

The Little Prince left the king for what he was and where he was—alone, without any control over him or anything else. This is how the Little Prince freed himself from the judgment of the king, of others, of this rat he had no use for: by ignoring the very existence of their power.

We are often very hard on ourselves when we look at the challenges we face and the errors we inevitably make. Yes, all of us are hard enough on ourselves without having to endure the judgment of others. I don't still have to ask myself to this day— yes or no?—am I ugly?

To free ourselves from the judgment of others is to erase this pseudo-power that would like to govern our existence, when we are all quite capable and clear-sighted enough to consciously judge our own acts.

TRAVEL DIARY

To grant power to another
is to put oneself at their mercy.

And my Little Prince told me . . .

He is free to be, the

one who never judges.

stop searching so you can start finding

LIKE THE LITTLE PRINCE

MAYBE YOU REMEMBER THIS from your own childhood. What has always struck me about children when they play together and invent stories with their action figures and dolls is what they do when the story is missing a prop. If a knight needs to arrive on horseback, and they don't have a horse on hand, do you know what they do? No?

Yes, of course you do: They change the story!

It is obvious to them: There is no horse? Okay, no problem, we'll do it differently! It is out of the question to put an end to a beautiful story just because of an unfortunate horse! The knight will instead arrive on a boat via the river that they have just created, winding between two cushions simulating mountains. This is much more than a child's game. In reality, it is an immense force, because they have adapted to the situation. They have not searched for a horse for hours, telling themselves that without it the story would be impossible; instead, they have found a solution so that the story continues.

If we transport this approach to our adult world, what would happen when a project, whether professional or personal, is missing a piece of the puzzle? We sometimes have the impression that everything must stop, that this small element is the keystone necessary for the completion of the project. We then focus on finding the missing piece, even if it does not exist, even if it is not necessarily indispensable, often forgetting the purpose of the project itself.

Removing the pebble in one's shoe becomes the objective. These situations always make me think of those robots that run straight into a wall, hit it, go back two yards and run again, and so on ad infinitum, without seeing that ten inches away there is an opening in the wall. The Little Prince is quite right: When we don't know what we're looking for, when we've lost the thread of the story for the children, or the goal of the project for the adults, we turn in circles. Our adult eyes are not able to see a solution. The infernal circle of our thoughts runs in a loop, and we don't know where to look, what to look for, and even less what we're trying to find.

Children bypass the difficulties in their stories with ease in order to bring them to happy conclusions. How do they do it?

It's quite simple: They are open to any option, any possibility. In sum, they are creative.

When things don't work out the way they want, they don't look for an accessory with their eyes, but rather for a solution with their heart, because it is the heart that drives them to tell their story. This is not a reasoned creative process, it is an instinctive creative process, because for them the most important thing is to meet the needs of the story, no matter how.

Remember those whispers in your room . . .

"Yes, but we said he was going to kill the bad guy with his axe."

"Yes, but actually, he was a student of a great wizard, so he can send fireballs! See, like this!"

"Oh yeah! That's great! That way he can still kill the bad guy . . ."

It is at times so disarming to see the infinite powers of children and what we lost as we grew up. When we try to compensate for imagination and creativity with knowledge, we often find that there is a piece missing for every project throughout our lives. Perhaps it is time to reconnect with the creative magic of the children we once were.

Perhaps it is time to find a solution to a problem, to find what we are made for, to find the person we are; perhaps it is time to stop searching and instead start finding. Time to stop searching with reason and start finding with the heart, time to stop following logic and instead get in touch with what we are feeling. This is certainly one of the most beautiful lessons that the Little Prince, whom we all carry within us, whispers into our ears when he says: "Only children know what they are looking for."

It is up to us to hear him, to truly listen to him.

Searching is not a quest,
when finding is the only end.

And my Little Prince told me . . .

I rarely found what I was looking for in the place where I was looking for it.

"And I love to listen to the stars at night. It's like five hundred million little bells . . ."

—THE AVIATOR

HOW TO

be free

LIKE THE LITTLE PRINCE

BATHING IN FREEDOM IS TYPICAL of childhood. Children don't think about freedom, they live it without even knowing how to put a word to it.

Even if we are aware when we are young that our families and school environments are conditioned and governed by rules, we do not see them as obstacles to our freedom to live, but as rules to follow (more or less!). When we are children, like the Little Prince, we live freely without thinking about it. Free to do whatever we want, free to play, to sleep, to dream, to disappear into our imaginary worlds, free to say no, free not to listen, free to ignore something when we don't feel like doing it. Free to plan everything, to do everything, anywhere, with anyone, and whenever we want.

How many of us can claim to have maintained such a sense of freedom in our lives? I can see you shaking your head over there. As adults, only a few of us do not find ourselves chained to a number of obligations or impossibilities, voluntarily or involuntarily established over time.

As the fox said to the Little Prince: "*You become responsible forever for what you have tamed. You are responsible for your rose . . .*" Becoming responsible, as we age, is one of the necessary facts of life, but one that causes us to give up some of our freedom in return. We become a little more constrained and thus a little less free, but this is not necessarily a negative aspect of our existence. The responsibilities we have to our children, our spouses, our families, and our friends are all beneficial constraints in our lives, a bit like the family and school rules that a child must follow. These rules do not prevent children from being free in any way. Like those rules, the obligations that make up our lives must never result in a feeling of imprisonment. We must never feel trapped; if we do, it is time to question our obligations and constraints.

The value of freedom for the Little Prince is also expressed in his refusal to tie his sheep to a stake on his planet. He does not even understand the need for it. He refuses any form of imprisonment whatsoever, any deprivation of freedom. After all, remember: Whom did the Little Prince ask for permission to start his journey, his quest from planet to planet? No one. Whether this journey was real or imaginary, he set off in complete freedom to discover the stars and the inhabitants of other planets.

Who accounts for our actions as adults? Not many people. But sometimes there are people who take up such a place in our lives, who become intrusive to the point of sometimes dictating our every move. This is the moment when any freedom we have to be who we want to be begins to die. Being free, as the Little Prince experiences, albeit at times bitterly during his journey, sometimes means being alone. This is why he is in search of friends, not to chain himself down, but to be able to choose the conditions of his freedom, a freedom that will then become shared.

We all have a secret garden, just as children have an imaginary world, without borders, where they feel free. It is up to us to push aside the walls of this secret garden in order to welcome the people with whom we have decided to share our lives, those we have decided to tame, those we have decided to let ourselves be tamed by, and those we let inside to nurture our freedom.

TRAVEL DIARY

Being free means choosing.
Choosing your addiction, choosing to
tame, choosing your form of freedom.

And my Little Prince told me . . .

No one is free, but no one

would really want to be free.

"It's sad to forget a friend. Not everyone has had a friend."

—THE AVIATOR

HOW TO

accept being misunderstood

LIKE THE LITTLE PRINCE

"YOU CAN'T PLEASE EVERYONE," the saying goes. But it is often not so much a question of pleasing as of being understood.

In this passage, it is the narrator, a.k.a. the aviator, who is speaking. He becomes aware of a dream that was stolen from him as a child, a dream that would have created a life that satisfied him. However, crossing paths with many people, for whom he had to alter his speech, and his desires, left him with the bitter taste of the child he once was, when he was never understood through his drawings and his imagination.

In adulthood, when a part of ourselves has remained perched in the sweetness of childhood reveries and imagination, we often find ourselves surrounded by those who prevent us from dreaming. Sometimes we have an idea or a project that escapes the sensibility or the understanding of the people to whom we explain it. Which is a terrible thing for the dreamers among us.

After all is said and done, there is one thing to remember: to accept that sometimes you will be misunderstood, and to keep the child within you and your desires all to yourself, especially when the audience isn't open to your musings.

To accept being misunderstood is to not pay attention to the sound of criticism, to not give in to the echo of mockery, to not bend under the weight of injunctions that define what is the acceptable or correct way of functioning. To accept being misunderstood means listening only to yourself, following your heart, and responding to your needs. It means letting yourself dream and making yourself smile. It is not useful to try to convince a reluctant audience of your good faith by holding out a stick for them to beat you with.

A little saying that comes to mind that applies to this subject is: "You can be misunderstood a thousand times by one person or once by a thousand people, but you don't want to be misunderstood a thousand times by a thousand people." Accepting being misunderstood allows us to disarm those who disparage our dreams. Even with the best of intentions, you must always be aware that you will never be able to convince everyone, to be understood by everyone, to be followed by everyone. In the end, accepting being misunderstood means allowing yourself to follow your dreams, your projects, and what is in your heart without having to hide, to stay silent, or to bow your head to the critics who often have nothing in common other than not having any dreams themselves.

I have never heard an entrepreneur, an artist, or an inventor mock or sabotage another creator's project, even if it was not his field. Dreamers listen to and help other dreamers because they know the difficulty of what it means to take on a seemingly impossible challenge and work hard at it, and they know the price of accepting being misunderstood. Be one of those dreamers, be one of those misunderstood creators, because then it is your sun that you will be shining across the world.

TRAVEL DIARY

Never deny the child you were;
continue to live beside them.

And my Little Prince told me . . .

**Look for common ground,
when everyone else is looking
to raise a fist.**

HOW TO

see beyond what is real and embrace the invisible

LIKE THE LITTLE PRINCE

MAGIC. MAGIC WAS OUR ONLY TRUTH, our only religion when we were children. Everything was magic, and the faith we had in its power allowed us to believe in everything, to see beyond the real world, far from the world of adults.

Nothing was impossible in our world. The faith we had in the magic that surrounded us allowed us to envision the invisible and to make our wishes come true. We were children, we were magical, and gazing up at the stars, we still knew how to see the treasures hidden on any planet simply by pointing up to it in the sky, hoping one day to discover its beauty. We knew that beyond the horizon, somewhere in the vast ocean, there was an island just for us with hidden treasures waiting to be discovered.

It is the invisible aspect of things that makes them attractive. Things visible on the surface concern only the world of adults. Adults who count, who quantify, who measure. And a surface that is palpable, computable, identifiable, reassuring, and comfortable. But does this surface aspect of things, of people, of the world around us, truly make us happy? When there is nothing else to aspire to or to discover other than what is displayed out in the open for all to see?

We have all experienced this at one time or another. On the surface, things may seem idyllic, but if there is nothing more below, it is like a flimsy postcard someone has sent us. A postcard that we file away while we await the next one, or quickly grow tired of and toss out, never to think of again.

This is also true for people who are so superficial that their plastic exterior hides the emptiness of their intellect and their souls, whose perfect bodies are like empty boxes, transporting them from one place to another, with nothing inside.

In everything there is a quest, in everything there is a treasure, in everything there is a discovery, and therein lies the true value, the magical part of everything. To refuse to imagine the magic, to glimpse it, to decide to confine oneself to a cold and Cartesian way of looking at the world only brings sadness and weariness to our lives and the world around us. To try to see beyond what is real, beyond the appearance of people and our reality, is to open ourselves to the possibility of discovering and marveling at everything again. It is to repeat over and over again with wild hope: What if? . . . What if? . . . What if? . . .

And from these questions, from these emerging possibilities, let the smile of the child seen in the other side of the mirror—the other side of all that is possible—reflect on your own face.

In truth, are our lives so exciting that we can't envision that part of the mystery, the unreal, and the projection that the child within us can offer? I should hope that we can—just imagine the wonders that would await you if you were to once again look at the world through the eyes of a child and agree to let the imaginary and the magic enter your life with open arms.

Growing up is no fun. Especially if, along the way, we forget how magical the world can be. As the aviator said of the Little Prince: "My friend never gave explanations. Perhaps he thought I was like him. But I, unfortunately, cannot see the sheep through the crates. Maybe I'm a bit like the grown-ups. I must have grown old."

For us to see the sheep through the crate again is the Little Prince's goal, namely to bring this touch of pure magic back into our lives.

Next to the front door is a shoebox. As I look at it, I think I can hear "Baa, baa . . ."

TRAVEL DIARY

Magic is the flavor of our lives,
the true color of the world.

And my Little Prince told me . . .

To try to see beyond the appearance of our reality is to open ourselves to the possibility of discovering and marveling at everything. Again.

HOW TO

change our standards of judgment

LIKE THE LITTLE PRINCE

IT WAS SO EASY TO BOND spontaneously when we were children, as I mentioned in a previous chapter. A few seconds of shyness led to a flowing exchange filled with laughter and with no regard for appearances.

When we became adults, we not only lost this ease, but we also added a whole list of judgment criteria that has only become longer and longer over the years. The Little Prince is quite right to point a finger at how adults gauge the world, often seeing objects, beauty, and people only from a quantifiable, measurable, rational point of view.

Is this person "bankable"?

Is this painting, which mesmerizes us with its colors, a masterpiece? Or is the way we perceive its beauty determined only by its monetary value? It is a good question to ask as we observe the parade of visual aberrations that modern art offers up as masterly beauties. It would be interesting to see what value people would place on certain works of art without knowing who made them or how much they are said to be worth. A bit of forbidden truth.

These judgment criteria are how, as adults, we assess many things and many people. They reassure us, in our relationships, in our career, and in our inner circles. At first glance, according to a person's attitude, clothing, signs of poverty or wealth, his or her car keys, the color of his or her credit card, we already have an image, an opinion about that person. We know, "thanks" to these criteria, which we have skillfully mastered over the course of our experiences and encounters, whether this person corresponds to those we are used to. We are not sure if we are from the same social or professional background, but before we even think of making a connection with this person, of trying to meet him or her, our automatic appraisals take over, allowing or forbidding us to take a step further.

This is sometimes very useful, I agree, and of course we cannot act and evolve in society like a giggling newborn baby wading in a bath of naivety. Nevertheless, the Little Prince's invitation to learn how to judge according to other criteria can be really useful to us.

With our lists of criteria, which we make longer with each new life experience, where is there room for astonishment and novelty? This is the limit of the system developed by us adults: We end up locking ourselves into a system that is too rigid, a perfectly defined universe in terms of comfort, behavior, and shared values. The codes are fixed, nothing new can pass through the gates, except what we know, what satisfies us, but which ends up confining us in a bubble of boredom.

We are all thirsty for astonishment and discovery; we are all digging for gold in our lives. But how can we still find a few golden nuggets, among the muddy thickness of the sand, if the sieve that is our minds no longer lets anything through?

So should we try to judge according to values other than the ones we are used to the next time we meet someone? Why not? In the end, it doesn't take much effort to simply remain open-minded, embrace the unfamiliar, and stay curious so that one day we may perhaps discover, with great astonishment, a new golden nugget of happiness.

While money has become our ultimate value and the basis of all decisions we make, we must never lose sight of the fact that money is only a measure of what is visible and ephemeral, not of true wealth.

Does parading bling around to "look like someone" make us happier? Does judging bling as a peremptory opinion without considering any possible alternatives make us happier?

"It is only with the heart that one can see rightly. What is essential is invisible to the eye," the fox tells us. This is the secret he passes on to the Little Prince, and which he in turn offers us. Perhaps it is up to us, starting today, to question some of our certainties,

our opinions, our arbitrary judgments, and our preconceived notions to break free of our "truth bubble" and once again marvel at the surprises along the way, like so many delicacies in life.

TRAVEL DIARY

Our judgment criteria are only our criteria of confinement.

And my Little Prince told me . . .

Gold never shines at the

bottom of a salt mine.

"It is so mysterious, the land of tears."
—THE AVIATOR

believe and stay hopeful

LIKE THE LITTLE PRINCE

"SO, WHAT DO YOU THINK? Are the stars lit up so that everyone can one day find their own?" All the hope of the world lies in the aviator's question. True faith is staying hopeful even when the walls close in and hide the brightness of the stars.

When I was five years old, suffering from a serious illness whose outcome seemed very uncertain for the years to come, I spent weeks in bed in the hospital, unable to move. I will spare you the details of the many troubling effects of the disease, but I still remember them. The disease was rare and somewhat unknown, with no possible treatment, and I had to wait to see how things would play out. One day, my grandmother came back from Lourdes, a town in southwest France, and brought a bottle of holy water to the hospital for me. The bottle was shaped like a heart, and she told me that if I drank a drop of the water every day, I would be cured.

And so I did. I took one sip a day, because the bottle was not very big, so the water level dropped quickly. With each sip of the water, I was sure to be cured, both by the power of the bottle and by the power of the water. I say "both" because after a few days, I realized that the bottle was being secretly refilled. I didn't say anything at the time. It wasn't important, because once the water was in the bottle, it became magical and healed me. I was sure of it. Oh, the power of childhood . . .

If I am still standing and writing these lines for you today, it is also for this reason. It is always about believing, believing in healing, keeping the faith in anything and everything until the magic happens.

The bottle was my shining star as a child. A star that promised me that one day I would escape those hospital walls. And I did. Believing is a powerful tool, far beyond religion. The Little Prince believes in his star and believes that everyone has their own star too. Are we as deeply convinced as he is that this star exists? Can we continue to trust it even as soon as we take our first steps into adulthood?

For some, yes. For others, the star has disappeared because they no longer believe in it. And yet, the greatest figures in history, whatever their field, have, at one time or another, evoked a deep faith, a belief that they had in themselves, in life, in a god. It doesn't matter what they believed in. Just like my bottle, imperturbable faith is all we need to keep going even in the worst situations.

Some of you who are reading this right now may have lost hope . . . maybe it's time to look up and find your star.

What if you let yourself be supported by this strength you had as a child, but that you may have since suppressed? What do you have to lose by still believing that everything is possible? Who can stop you from believing in yourself, in life, in the hope that the best is yet to come? What dogma, what rule, what principle can stand in your way?

Only you, your desire, your courage, and your faith can reach your shining star. To look up at the sky is to look inside yourself to find the child within you still clinging to your star.

TRAVEL DIARY

Whatever happens is always what is
best for us. No matter what happens,
there is always a star.

And my Little Prince told me . . .

**I am still holding on to this star,
to this crazy hope of one day
becoming someone else.**

leave, let go, and not be alone

LIKE THE LITTLE PRINCE

IT IS ALWAYS HARD TO KNOW when to leave, even if it tears us apart. It is hard to know how to leave when, like the Little Prince, it becomes clear that it is time to pursue a life path somewhere else.

Leaving is often not a decision, but a necessity in life that pushes us in a direction, without us seeing the destination clearly in front of us. Leaving to follow one's path is necessary, even if it means leaving loved ones behind for a while.

There is no point in fighting it, because then you are fighting against yourself. We all must follow a path—we don't have a choice about that. But we do have a choice about which path we follow, and when it becomes clear what our choice should be, we must act. We can postpone the moment of departure and extend the pain of staying and the fear of leaving, but in reality, when the moment arrives, there is no other choice.

It is necessary to know how to leave when it is time, at any age, if for no reason other than the motivation that still inspires us to never lose the candor of the child we once were even as we grow older.

We must also know how to let go when it is time. Our loved ones, or our children, may be called to head overseas, or to leave for their studies, a job, or a love story. If we really love them, we must let them go, even with tears in our eyes, because their happiness in life depends on it. What else can we wish for those we love? What more beautiful gesture of love can we give?

The fox is proof that, even when we say goodbye, our loved ones can remain in our hearts through reminders of their existence. For example, the wheat fields take on new meaning for the fox as their color reminds him of the Little Prince's golden curls.

The Little Prince's quest led him to meet new people, and to experience new things, but above all it led him to connect with others and make friends, so that he would never again feel alone on his planet. It takes so much to create one's own world, and in this world, anything can happen. But this does not mean that one must accept everything that happens, under the pretext of wanting to belong to a group and have only pseudo-friends. This is how the Little Prince sought and chose his friends and why he didn't bond with the businessman or the drunkard. This is why, surrounded by his volcanoes and his flower, even far from the fox, he knows he will never be alone again when he looks up at the stars.

We too are alone at times on our planet. And yet, there are no "friendship dealers" for adults, there are only friendships whose strength is based on our inner child's soul, in its most sincere form, without any stakes, without competition, without calculation.

Friendship is the only true relationship based on equality that exists. It has a price, that of our childlike soul, that of our sincerity.

And, just like with the fox, separation and differences never prevent true friendship, as long as we always remember the color of the wheat.

TRAVEL DIARY

Don't expect life to give you answers,
but rather a path to follow.

And my Little Prince told me . . .

Make a wish that you discover
that beyond sight there is
vision, that vision leads to truth,
and that truth conceals the will
of life.

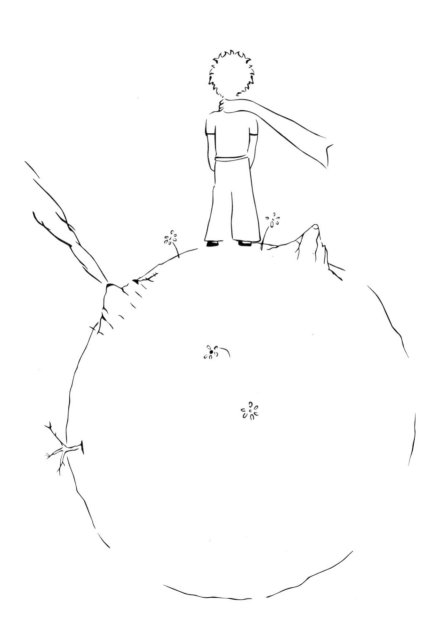

get back on your cloud

LIKE THE LITTLE PRINCE

IN THE SECTION TITLED "On a Cloud," at the beginning of this book, I quoted Saint-Exupéry's dedication as a guideline: *"All grown-ups were once children . . . but only a few of them remember it."*

As I climb back onto my cloud after having traveled through the intricacies of the Little Prince's doubts and questions, wanting to reconnect with my soul and my childlike outlook, I can only respond to this dedication with this sentence from chapter 2 of *The Little Prince*: "Children should always show great forbearance toward grown-ups." Maybe this is how we continue our personal development today: by knowing how to listen and showing great tolerance toward those grown-ups who have forgotten their childhood souls.

And by making a wish once again, making a wish to one day grow big enough to know how to reach out to this child who never leaves our heart, who never abandons their dreams and their sweetness, this child that we all remain, despite the time that passes by.

And my Little Prince told me . . .

Pay attention to the wishes you grant; they come true.

IN THE MIRROR,

can you see the Little Prince deep inside of you?

CAN THE LITTLE PRINCE WITHIN us be reborn in this game of mirrors?

Yes, if we really want it.

Yes, if we really believe in it.

Perhaps we just need to ask ourselves two questions in all sincerity to see him poke his head into the corner of the mirror: "What are the most important dreams and who are the most important people in your life today?"

Now compare these dreams with the dreams from your childhood that you wrote down on page 13 of this book. Are there any similarities, any commonalities? Did some dreams come true? Do others, which seemed to be impossible desires in the past, still excite you today?

Bring the past and present together.

What comes out of it? What have you achieved, what do you cherish, what do you still dream of experiencing in your life? Now, jot each of these thoughts in a small personal notebook that will be your own travel diary. For each of these elements, projects, or people that you cherish, note what you do or what you could do to take care of them, to nurture them even more than you do today.

They are the keys to your happiness, the whisper of the Little Prince inside of you.

Believe in yourself, believe in the dreams that your Little Prince is whispering in your ear, all that he can offer you once again.

It may just be that, by looking up at the stars one evening, the planets will align—yours and your Little Prince's—as if by magic.

notes